HIRED!

Everything you need to know about getting a job.

Leading you through the process of resumes, interviews, salary negotiation, letters of resignation, and more.

by Mayya Bower

TABLE OF CONTENTS

Introduction 2
CHAPTER 1: *The Resume* 2
    HEADER 3
    YOUR OBJECTIVE 4
    SKILLS 7
    EDUCATION 8
    WORK EXPERIENCE 9
    RESEARCH EXPERIENCE 11
    OTHER 11
    REFERENCES UPON REQUEST 11
CHAPTER 2: *The Cover Letter* 16
    COVER LETTER RULES 17
    FORMATTING THE COVER LETTER 19
CHAPTER 3: *Salary Requirements* 24
    CONSIDER YOUR COST OF LIVING EXPENSES 25
CHAPTER 4: *The Interview* 26
    PREPARE FOR THE INTERVIEW 26
    ANSWERING INTERVIEW QUESTIONS 29
    ASK QUESTIONS 35
    WRAPPING UP 35
    8 WAYS TO HAVE A SUCCESSFUL INTERVIEW 35
    REFLECT 38
CHAPTER 5: *175 Possible Interview Questions You May Encounter* 40
CHAPTER 6: *Answering Interview Questions* 50
CHAPTER 7: *73 Questions To Ask The Interviewer* 77

CHAPTER 8: *Thank You Letters* 83
    FORMATTING A THANK YOU EMAIL 83
    FORMATTING A THANK YOU NOTE 85
CHAPTER 9: *Following Up* 87
    EMAIL 88
    PHONE CALLS 89
CHAPTER 10: *Job Offers & Negotiations* 91
    CONSIDERING AN OFFER 92
    DECLINING AN OFFER 93
CHAPTER 11: *Organizing The Search* 95
CHAPTER 12: *Places to Search* 97
CHAPTER 13: *Letter of Resignation* 99
CHAPTER 14: *Informational Interviewing* 101
    WHY GO THROUGH THE HASSLE? 101
    SCHEDULING THE INTERVIEW 103
CHAPTER 15: *Gaining Experience While In College* 115
CHAPTER 16: *Finding Opportunities in Rejection* 119

Introduction

There are many strategies, protocols, and procedures that become valuable knowledge when you are entering or exiting the job market. With this step-by-step guide, you will navigate through all the employment opportunity process without missing a beat.

I want you to get the most out of this guide. You can use this book as a reference guide for each step of the job-seeking process. Go through this page by page, or skip to the chapter that you need. The goal is to equip you with all of the necessary tools to land the job want.

No more worries and no more fears. You may be on a journey to places you've not yet discovered in the job market, but this guide will help you steer clear of common mistakes that lead to missed opportunities. Instead, you will find yourself successfully maneuvering through the endless possibilities available today.

CHAPTER 1

The Resume

This is where it all begins. Yes, you will probably have to fill out a tedious application online, but having a strong resume will help you save time when you start to copy and paste it into the appropriate sections. Some places will consider the resume to be like an introduction of who they may consider for hire while others will look at the resume as validation that a potential hire is capable of fulfilling the position. When it comes down to it, you've got to have an easy-to-read document with all of the right buzzwords.

When employers are trying to fill a position, their goal is to find the best candidate as quickly as possible. When you submit a captivating resume you make the process easier for the employer.

Oftentimes, this can be the hardest to do when looking for a job. When attempting to put together a resume for the first time or compiling the necessary information, it can take a lot of time and effort, not to mention there are so many ways to go about it.

The key to remember is that you are focusing on selling yourself. The individuals who are hiring you don't know you, so you have to make yourself shine! You do this by talking up your experiences, capabilities, and potential.

HEADER

Begin with your name on the top using large, bold, print so that it stands out. Stick with simple fonts like: Arial, Courier New, Georgia, Times New Roman, Trebuchet, or Verdana. The header of your resume (your name) can be a large size, but keep the rest of your resume between 10 and 12 point. Following your name is your contact information, including address, phone, and email.

> **💡 QUICK TIPS 💡**
> - If you are looking to relocate, leave your current address out. Companies view relocation assistance differently, which can be a point of discussion for the future. Or, you may not even bring that point up and pay for relocation on your own.
> - Before you start sending out emails, be sure you create a conventional email which includes your name rather than any nicknames. Keep your email address for job applications conservative, such as your first and last name, or initials with numbers.

YOUR OBJECTIVE

Next is your objective. Most often the objective statement includes 1-3 line of text, summarizing the position(s) you are applying for and/or your main qualifications. To improve your chances for success, it is always a good idea to tailor your objective statement to a particular organizations or position. That means you may need to adjust your objective if you are applying for different jobs that are in unrelated fields.

Avoid making objective statements that are too general or vague, such as "an internship allowing me to utilize my knowledge and expertise in different areas." This type of statement does not let the reader know what your knowledge or expertise are. Instead, you want to cause the person reviewing your resume to visualize you in the position you desire by showing you already have some idea of what it entails.

Questions to Ask Yourself
It is often difficult to write an objective that will stand out from the competition so use the following questions as guide to help you.
1) *What are your main qualifications such as strengths, skills, and areas of expertise?*
2) *What positions or range of positions are you seeking?*
3) *What are your professional goals?*
4) *What type of organization or work setting are you interested in?*
5) *Which of your qualifications are most desired by the ones who will be reading your resume?*

6) *What position titles (or range of positions) are available?*
7) *What are some goals of the organization that interest you?*
8) *What types of organizations or work settings are now hiring?*

FILL IN THE BLANK
If you are unsure on what to write, use the following templates by filling the blank.

If you know or want to emphasize a specific position (or two) and your main relevant qualifications, you might experiment with one or more of these formats:
1. *A position as a <u>name or type of position</u> allowing me to use my <u>list of up to 3 qualifications</u>.*
2. *To utilize my <u>list of up to 3 qualifications</u> as a <u>position title</u>.*

If you know or want to emphasize the field or type of organization you want to work in and your professional goal or your main qualifications, you might experiment with one or more of these formats:
1. *An opportunity to <u>professional goal</u> in a <u>type of organization, work environment, or field</u>.*
2. *To enter <u>type of organization, work environment, or field</u> allowing me to use my <u>list of up to 3 qualifications</u>.*

If you know or want to emphasize your professional or career goal or an organizational

goal, you might experiment with one or more of these formats:
1. To _professional goal._
2. An opportunity to _professional goal._

> **Word Replacement**
> Words can be influential and impactful in any given situation, one of which is when building your resume.
>
> Something that will enable you to build a better resume is to write out all the necessary information and then go back and replace common words with substitutions.
>
> Substituting words like **use** with words like **develop**, **apply**, or **employ**.
>
> Replacing **allowing me** with **requiring** or **giving me the opportunity**.
>
> Changing **enter** to **join**, **pursue**, **obtain**, **become a member**, and **contribute**.
>
> These are just some of the ways you can increase the weight of your words. You can also use Google by searching for the word followed by "synonym" to find replacements for something specific. Remember to use vocabulary that makes sense with the job you are after and that paints a clear picture of you as a valuable team player who is an ideal hire.

SKILLS

As a recently graduated student, it will be all the more important that you list your skills. Often times you would not have the work experience the employer may be looking for therefore it is critical that you make yourself stand out with a strong skill set. Depending on what work area you are going into will determine how you will tailor the skills section, and your entire resume for that matter.

Your skill section should be a mix of both hard skills, which are technical and learned, and soft skills, which are more people and behavior focused.

The following is a list of some of the top hard and soft skills to consider adding to your resume:

Top 10 Hard Skills	Top 10 Soft Skills
Data Analysis	Data Analysis
Copywriting	Copywriting
Foreign Languages	Foreign Languages
Accounting	Accounting
Computer Languages	Computer Languages
Mathematics	Mathematics
Graphic Design	Graphic Design
Planning / Event Planning	Planning / Event Planning
SEO / SEM Marketing	SEO / SEM Marketing
Bookkeeping	Bookkeeping

EDUCATION

It is important that you add your education on your resume to showcase the type of knowledge and skill set you are coming into the workforce with. There are two methods of showcasing that information.

If you have already graduated and received your degree, you can use the following template:

<u>College</u> - <u>Area of Study</u>, <u>Degree Level</u>
Example: University - Communications, BA

If you are anticipating graduation and are trying to get ahead of the game, you can use this template:
<u>College</u> - <u>Area of Study</u>, <u>Degree Level</u> (Expected: <u>Month</u> <u>Year</u>)
Example: University - Communications, BA (Expected May 2020).

If you attended any technical schools or gained additional technical training elsewhere, be sure to include that on your resume. Include the training program you completed as well as any certifications that were gained along the way.

WORK EXPERIENCE

If you have not been working in the field, industry, or job you have your sights on, that doesn't mean you can't include that information. Companies consider how well you are able to balance your workload with external factors. Additionally, by showcasing your successes rather than your responsibilities, you will be able to stand out from the crowd.

Begin your work experience with your current employer at the very top, and work your way down in descending chronological order, not to exceed ten years or one page. Include the name of the organization, location, your dates of hire in month/year format, and your title. A common format you may consider following is:
<u>Employer Name</u>, <u>City</u>, <u>State</u> <u>(Years of Employment)</u>
<u>Title</u>

Example: XYZ Co, Anywhere, KS (2014-Present)
   Receptionist

  Once the company and title information is complete, begin filling in the rest of the resume with your accomplishments. Anything you can quantify will work towards your advantage.
1. Did you receive employee of the month/year for doing something?
2. Did you implement new strategies?
3. Help train? How many?
4. Saved the company $X amount?
5. What were your sales numbers?
6. Customer satisfaction numbers?

The key is to showcase to the employer why you are a better candidate from the competition with quantifiable numbers to back it up. What makes you stand out from the other students who are graduating with you, working at the same place as you, with the same degree?

If you only remember the most recent 1 or 2 employers and your accomplishments, just list those and leave the rest with just the name of the company, location, years of employment, and your title.

Internships are critical in this section. If you successfully worked an internship, even for a semester, you gained critical skills for the workforce.

RESEARCH EXPERIENCE

This section may or may not come before your work experience, depending on the field you are trying to get into. However the format should follow the same as the work experience section. Be sure you include any published works or presentations you were part of.

OTHER

The following is a list of potential areas you might consider including in your resume, with the caveat of them being relevant to the job, organization, and/or industry that you are applying for.

- Volunteer experience
- Special certifications
- Proficient languages
- School accomplishments (such as members to honors societies or serving on boards)

REFERENCES UPON REQUEST

Conclude your resume with the "References Upon Request" statement at the very bottom. It is not necessary to provide your references as it will take up precious resume space. However, be sure you have all of your references ready to go on a seperate sheet should you be asked. Include information such as the person's first and last name, where you worked with them, their phone number, and possibly their email as well.

> ### 💡 QUICK TIPS 💡
> - As a new graduate, aim to keep your resume to one page. As your relevant experience begins to grow, so will your resume.
> - Personalize and customize your resume to the specific job you are trying to get.
> - Keep it all to one font type.
> - Avoid any extra graphics, scrolls, or colors for general, professional positions. If you are applying to a more creative role, your resume becomes a part of your portfolio.

When describing your experiences, use action verbs to help your statements stand out, such as these:

accelerate
advise
analyze
approve
arrange
assemble
assist
build
collect
complete
conceive
conduct
control
coordinate
create
delegate
detect
develop
direct
discover
distribute
edit
deliver
demonstrate
design
eliminate

expedite
formulate
generate
implement
improve
increase
influence
install
instruct
lead
maintain
manage
motivate
obtain
operate
order
organize
originate
oversee
participate
perform
pinpoint
plan
prepare
present
process
produce
program
promote
propose

protest
prove
provide
purchase
receive
recommend
record
reduce
reinforce
reorganize
represent
research
revamp
review
revise
schedule
select
sell
setup
solve
streamline
structure
study
supervise
support
teach
test
train
write

Having a hard time making your resume work for the job you want?

Check out http://online.onetcenter.org/

This site is a great tool that can give you an overview of any particular occupation you are aiming for and what knowledge, skills, and behaviors a company may look for in their candidates and employees.

If you have any of the qualifications listed, it would be beneficial for you to incorporate them into your resume and cover letter to help attract the right buzzwords.

CHAPTER 2

The Cover Letter

———◆———

This can oftentimes be the hardest item to create because just like your resume, you really have to sit down and think through it. Effective cover letters explain the reasons for your interest in the specific organization and identify your most relevant skills or experiences. They should express a high level of interest and knowledge about the position.

The power of the cover letter can be incredibly impactful. Rather than listing the facts, like you would with a resume, the cover letters allow you to express who you are as an individual.

After spending lots of time preparing your resume, you may feel like you are too busy to write a cover letter. The idea of more research and work can be exhausting when all you want to do is get a job quickly. Don't allow the difficulty of the process to cause you to miss out on the impact the process produces.

COVER LETTER RULES

RULE #1: ALWAYS SEND A COVER LETTER

The first rule of cover letter etiquette is to send a cover letter -- always. It doesn't matter if the hiring manager asked for it or not. Unless the ad specifically states no cover letter -- send one. The cover letter is effective and could be the one element that sets you apart.

RULE #2: GET TO THE POINT

The recruiter or manager who is reading your application is likely looking through several resumes. Write your cover letter in such a way that respects their time.

When you get directly to the point and eliminate the unnecessary jargon, it demonstrates discipline, decisiveness, and efficiency, all of which are desired traits in a future employee. Be sure to break up any paragraphs that are seven links or longer into short, easily digestible ones. When your cover letter and resume are easy to read and to the point, you equip the hiring manager with all the necessary information needed to make a wise decision and eliminating the frustration of reading material filled with fluff.

RULE #3: AVOID "COMMON KNOWLEDGE" LANGUAGE

At one time it may have been a great idea to send an email that included such statements as: "Please see attached resume." "Thank you for your time and consideration." Although there is nothing wrong with saying those statements and it is always a good idea to be thankful, but general statements like that can also lose the power of their purpose by overuse and familiarity. With today's general understanding of email, it would be better to assume the individual is capable of finding the attachment.

RULE #4: SPRINKLE IN A LITTLE PERSONALITY
As it has already been stated, it is important that you are direct and to the point when writing your cover letter. However, cover letters also give you a chance to reveal your personality. Using a friendly and professional tone can help endear you to the hiring manager. Think through your writing and look at it from the perspective of the person who is hiring, but has no knowledge of who you are and what you are like. Then reread it from the same perspective to ensure your personality comes through clear, evident, and positive. Consider having a friend or family member read the cover letter to see if it is conveying the message you are trying to send. You don't have to be afraid of adding the friendly tone, just be sure to lower your risk of sounding unprofessional by taking the time to be intentional with every thought and word. Most importantly, <u>avoid using slang, acronyms, jokes, or puns</u>.

RULE #5: ADDRESS IT TO A SPECIFIC PERSON
Whenever possible, address your cover letter to a specific person. If a job posting doesn't include a person's name, do some research to find out who the correct person is to address. One of the quickest and easiest ways is to search the company's website. If that doesn't result with anything, go on to LinkedIn. Be sure you are taking correct and precise notes during your research so you do not put the wrong name or company information on the letter.

Keep the salutations professional by using "Dear Mr/Mrs" and avoid referring to the individual by a nickname, such as Jim in place of James.

While you're researching names in the company, be sure you also research what problems the organization may be facing. Discover the issues and struggles they are looking to overcome and present yourself, your skills, and your experiences in such as that you are the answer to their problems. Organizations with problems are eager to hire problem solvers.

RULE #6: EMPLOY A LITTLE CREATIVITY
A stand out cover letter increases your chances of always landing on top of the pile of potential hires, especially if you employ some creativity. Consider including a very brief summary of a tough sale or most challenging project to reveal how you succeeded or grew from the experience.

RULE #7: PROOFREAD, PROOFREAD, PROOFREAD
Cover letters, and resumes, should be free of errors. As qualified as you may be for the opening, you're likely to fall out of contention if your cover letter is full of typos, misspellings and grammatical errors. Ask friends and family to review your document to make sure there are no mistakes.

FORMATTING THE COVER LETTER

Now let's look at the breakdown of the cover letter.

First Paragraph - Why you are writing?
Your opening paragraph should capture the reader's attention. Rather than simply saying, "I am applying for the copywriter

position posted on AnytownPaper.com," follow up with, "Your need for an experienced professional is a good match for my five years of experience in advertising and extensive copywriting background. "If you've been referred to the hiring manager, be sure to point out the mutual contact in your lead. This may encourage the person to read further.

When it comes to writing cover letters, you can take one of three approaches:

1) *Referral:* A friend or acquaintance may have referred you to a potential employer. Be sure to mention this mutual contact, by name, up front since it is likely to encourage your reader to keep reading.
2) *Response to a job posting:* indicate where you learned of the position and the title of the position. More importantly, express your enthusiasm and the likely match between your credentials and the position's qualifications.
3) *A prospecting letter* (a letter in which you inquire about possible job openings): state your specific job objective. Since this type of letter is unsolicited, it is even more important to capture the reader's attention.

Second Paragraph - What do you have to offer?
Refer specifically to the qualifications listed and illustrate how your particular abilities and experiences relate to the position for which you are applying. In a prospecting letter express your potential to fulfill the employer's needs rather than focus on what the employer can offer you. You can do this by giving evidence that you have researched the organization thoroughly and that you possess skills used within that organization.

Focus on aspects of your background that relate directly to the job opportunity and note any relevant accomplishments, training, classes or certifications. The cover letter also allows you to explain anything that might be unclear or questionable on your resume, such as a gap in employment or change in career paths.

Give hiring managers a compelling reason to call you in for an interview. Instead of saying you have strong communication skills, provide examples: "I recently led a training session in the sales department on a new database application and received significant praise for my ability to relay complex information to a non-tech-oriented audience."

Third Paragraph - How you will follow up?
Close by reiterating your interest in the job and letting the employer know how they can reach you. It's easy for cover letters and resumes to become separated, so make sure hiring managers can reach you should they only have your cover letter. Be certain to include your phone number and email address.

Emphasize your achievements and problem-solving skills. Show how your education and work skills are transferable, and thus relevant, to the position for which you are applying. While you want to sell your qualifications, don't forget to explain how you would add value to the company. If your cover letter is dominated by "I," chances are you need to focus more of your content on the prospective employer.

Once all has been created and sent, confirm that your materials were received and that your application is complete. Some of the best efforts have been foiled due to a lack of follow up. You have to walk the fine line between no follow up and outright annoying. Be careful not to waste time by falling prey to follow up overload, but also remember it is the squeaky wheel the gets the grease.

CHAPTER 3
Salary Requirements

Sometimes when applying for jobs, an employer may request a salary history or salary requirements. This is generally asked for upfront so that the company is able to quickly determine if they can afford you based on the budget they have to work with. The most common way of including your salary requirement is in your cover letter. You may state it in terms of negotiation: "My salary requirement is negotiable based upon the job responsibilities and the total compensation package," or a range: "My salary requirement is in the $25,000 - $35,000 range."

To prepare for the salary requirements conversation, be sure you do some research. Be honest with the outcome, considering both your education <u>and</u> your years of experience as well as where you live. Sites such as www.salary.com and www.payscale.com are good places to start what the going rate is.

CONSIDER YOUR COST OF LIVING EXPENSES

Determine your salary requirements by looking at what your current costs are. Consider your bills, cost of living, and basic needs on a monthly basis. Then multiply that figure by 12 to find out how much you need each year to maintain your current standard of living. And don't forget to factor in those student loans!

If you are considering moving somewhere else, do plenty of research to determine how much the cost of living is on average: rent, utilities, groceries, transportation, and social events. Compare all of these numbers to where you currently live to better understand what salary range you will need to be at.

Be thoughtful of all the details concerning your finances before you apply for a job. It would not be good for your work history to land a job, only to then find out it doesn't pay enough and have to leave right away. In the same manner that you would research the place you are looking to work for to create a dynamic resume, research your financial needs.

The process of determining the salary you need may also help to eliminate places that cannot pay such a salary. While this will narrow your options, making it more difficult and more competitive to get the job, it will also simplify the target areas allowing you to focus more intently on the place you hope to work.

CHAPTER 4
The Interview

After countless hours of researching and sending out your resume to prospective employers, you've finally landed the interview. First and foremost, research the company -- ALWAYS. Understand who you will be working for and what they're gaps are.

PREPARE FOR THE INTERVIEW

Depending on what interview round you are on will determine what objectives you will be needing to meet.

> **ROUND ONE**
> **Your objectives are:**
> 1. Make a good impression.
> 2. Determine if you are interested in pursuing the position further.

> 3. Receive an invitation for a second interview if you are interested in pursuing the position further.
>
> **The interviewer's objectives will be:**
> 1. Obtain information to determine whether you have the skills and qualifications to do the job.
> 2. Determine who to invite back for a second interview.
> 3. Determine if you will be a good cultural fit for the company, the team, and essentially their management style.

> **ROUND TWO (OR THREE, FOUR…)**
> **Your objectives are to:**
> 1. Obtain more information about the company and position to determine if you are interested in pursuing the job further
> 2. Impress the interviewer(s) and receive a job offer
>
> **The interviewer's objectives are to:**
> 1. Introduce you to other people to see if there is a "fit" between you and the company and/or team.
> 2. Probe further into any areas where they want more information (NOTE: You may actually go through 3, 4 or more rounds of interviews prior to receiving any job offer).

When you are asked back for a second interview it means that you are considered a viable candidate for the position and you are qualified to do the job. Second interviews vary with each company. Since you are going to meet with different people, you can expect to be asked some of the same questions, beginning with "Tell me about yourself," or "Walk me through your resume."

They know you have the skills by now, and will be looking to see personality and cultural fit. You will be measured against other candidates who have applied for the same position. It is important that you leave the interviewer with something to make you remembered. Think of five strengths you have and pick the one that you feel differentiates you from the pack. An example would be a technical person who has great customer service skills.

Questions for the 2nd interview can also center around the particular challenges of the company and how you would be an asset in helping them, which is where your research and detective skills come in hand. The questions you ask will be determined by what was covered in the first interview. Information that you need to know, so that if you are offered the position, you can make a good choice for you, is:

- Exact specifications of the job: what will you be doing? (Then ask yourself "IS that what I want to do?")
- The expectations the company has for the person they hire. (Then ask "Are they realistic?" and "Do I think I can (or want to) meet those expectations?")

Your round 2 questions will begin to dig deeper into:
- Specifics about your supervisors

- How your past experience fits in with the work position and opportunities for growth
- Who will you be working with and how closely
- What territories does the company cover
- Does the company have plans for expansion and whether you will be responsible for doing any of the development
- What strategies have they used in the past
- What worked and did not
- Any analysis about why would be especially useful now

Other subjects may come up in this interview such as salary requirements and benefits. Prepare by doing some research on salary and thinking about your benefits requirements. You cannot negotiate a salary until you have an offer, but you can prepare by knowing the "going rate" for your position. You should also do a budget sheet of your expenses and figure out what it costs you to live each month. You should know your "walk away" number, when you cannot afford to take the job. Refer to chapter 3, Salary Requirements, to help walk you through this process.

ANSWERING INTERVIEW QUESTIONS

There will be a handful of questions that you will hear over and over again at just about every interview you go to. This chapter will walk you through the top five questions. Outside of these, there are hundreds of other questions you could get asked. Be sure you take some time to review the following chapters, 175 Interview Questions and Answering Interview

Questions, and come up with some answers that you can have on hand with you.

1. **Talking About Yourself**

   The interviewer is often trying to find out how you organize, your thinking, what you focus on, and how well you articulate your thoughts when you answer. Be sure to keep your answers concise and do not go off on tangents. Talk about professional and academic accomplishments and avoid personal topics. Keep it to a quick 2-3 minute snapshot of who you are and why you're the best candidate for the position.

   Example: "Well, first of all, I am pleased to be here meeting you because I have long been an admirer of your company and of the work you personally have done. I believe I have what you are looking for. I am currently working with ABC Corporation where I head the accounting team. I have 8 years experience in accounting and internal audit with two Fortune 500 companies. In my performance appraisals, my bosses have remarked that I am an effective contributor and a good problem solver and that I have an excellent ability to create and implement office procedures and systems. I would be happy to elaborate on any of these, if you would like me to."

2. **Discussing Your Strengths**

   This is one of the easier interview questions you'll be asked. It is important to discuss attributes that will qualify you for the job. Describe the skills and experiences that directly correlate with the job you are applying for. Highlight positive skills, like prioritization, problem-solving, working under pressure, focusing on projects, professional expertise, leadership skills, and/or a positive attitude.

For example:
- When I'm working on a project, I don't want just to meet deadlines. Rather, I prefer to complete the project well ahead of schedule.
- I have exceeded my sales goals every quarter and I've earned a bonus each year since I started with my current employer.
- My time management skills are excellent. I am organized, efficient, and take pride in excelling at my work.
- I pride myself on my customer service skills and my ability to resolve what could be difficult situations.

3. **Discussing Your Weaknesses**

Do not try to mention a strength and present is as a weakness. Trying to say that you are a workaholic or that you are a stickler for detail and using those as a weakness will make it seem that you are attempting to dodge the question or over-glorify yourself. Talk about your weakness in content knowledge rather than a basic personal quality or skill. A lack of content knowledge is much easier to fix than a personality trait.

For example, saying that you are unfamiliar with a computer software rather than saying you have difficulty managing people. You should also mention what you are doing to remedy the weakness.

4. **Prioritizing Work**
   Consider answering this question one of two ways:

   1. Prioritize based on most important and not by who has seniority or who asked you first.
   2. For example: If you had a huge document to photocopy and collate for a meeting that was taking place in an hour and an urgent email to staff that needed to be sent right away and your boss wanted you to contact the travel agency and fix his tickets for this afternoon's flights. Which one would you do first and why?
   3. Review the length each assignment would take.
   4. For example, you have 3 projects and you know that 2 would take the least amount of time so you would knock those out first and then work on the 3rd project.

   If there are unequal factors, rank assignments by deadlines, time for each project, and seniority of person who requested the project.

5. **Explaining Terminations**
   This is often a very uneasy topic to discuss, but the best thing you can do is be 100% honest about the situation and explain how you have fixed such behaviors.

   For example:
   - Being cut loose was a blessing in disguise. Now I have an opportunity to explore jobs that better suit my qualifications and interests. My

research suggests that such an opportunity may be the one on your table. Would you like to hear more about my skills in working with new technology?

- My competencies were not the right match for my previous employer's needs but it looks like they'd be a good fit in your organization. In addition to marketing and advertising, would skills in promotion be valued here?
- Although circumstances caused me to leave my first job, I was very successful in school and got along well with both students and faculty. Perhaps I didn't fully understand my boss's expectations or why he released me so quickly before I had a chance to prove myself.
- The job wasn't working out so my boss and I agreed that it was time for me to move on to a position that would show a better return for both of us. So here I am, ready to work.
- After thinking about why I left, I realize I should have done some things differently. That job was a learning experience and I think I'm wiser now. I'd like the chance to prove that to you.
- A new manager came in and cleaned house in order to bring in members of his old team. That was his right but it cleared my head to envision better opportunities elsewhere.
- Certain personal problems, which I now have solved, unfortunately upset my work life. These problems no longer exist and I'm up and running strong to exceed expectations in my new job.

- I wanted my career to move in a different direction, and I guess my mental separation set up the conditions that led to my departure. But by contrast, the opportunity we're discussing seems to be made for me and I hope to eventually grow into a position of responsibility.
- My job was offshored to India. People familiar with my work say it is superior and fairly priced.
- I outlasted several downsizings but the last one included me. Sign of the times, I guess.
- I was desperate for work and took the wrong job without looking around the corner. I won't make that mistake again. I'd prefer an environment that is congenial, structured and team-oriented, where my best talents can shine and make a substantial contribution.

> **💡 QUICK TIPS 💡**
>
> - For every job or internship you have while you are in school, ask for a letter of recommendation from any or all of the people you report to or interact with. Ask that the letter be printed on letterhead and officially signed. Then, scan it in and/or make quality copies of the original. Bring the letter copies with you to your interviews.
> - Any of your experiences in the classroom can translate into answers for your interview. Team projects and extra activities are excellent sources to tap into.

For more ideas on how to answer interview questions, go to chapter 6, Answering Interview Questions.

ASK QUESTIONS

At the end of the interview, the interviewer will have some time for you to ask questions. Be sure you take the time to ask thoughtful questions that may not have been addressed during the interview. Prepare yourself by writing down some on your quick sheet to have on hand. Check out chapter 7, Questions to Ask the Interview, for a large list of possible questions to ask.

WRAPPING UP

Before getting up and shaking their hand, you want to talk about some of the things you have learned about the company, the work you may be doing, and mention how much you look forward to working with them. Also, be sure to ask for a business card if they have not already given you one.

8 WAYS TO HAVE A SUCCESSFUL INTERVIEW

1. <u>Arrive on time</u>. Be sure you are EARLY to the interview, but no more than by 15 minutes. This will give you opportunities to get a feel of the company and also make a good impression that you are eager to get the job. If you are too early, stay in your car or in a lobby area before walking up to be seen.

2. <u>Come prepared</u>. Be sure to research the company and understand the company's mission statement or basic workings. Know who you will be interviewing with by conducting a quick LinkedIn or Google search to get a great inside look. Bring extra copies of your resume and cover letter. Consider creating a quick sheet of information that is only available to you to list important points you want to touch on during the interview. Organize everything neatly into a folder or a professional padfolio, and bring a notebook or notepad to take notes on.

3. <u>Dress appropriately</u>. The rule of thumb is to dress one step up from the position or dress code of the company. If you are interviewing for a corporate-style position, consider wearing a suit or blazer with appropriate bottoms. If you don't have that, wear what you would on a daily basis to the job. If you are interviewing for a construction position, you would wear your safety boots, clean and neat jeans or work pants, and an appropriate work shirt. Also, leave the cologne/perfume at home.

- Iron your clothes. Rumpled and wrinkled clothes are not appropriate.
- Shoes should be moderately heeled, not scuffed, and coordinate with your outfit.
- Limit earrings to one per ear, or remove entirely.
- Do not wear jewelry that dangles, clangs, or is otherwise distracting
- Hands and nails should be trimmed. If you have chipped polish, remove it and go natural.
- **Dress not for where you are, but where you want to be**

4. <u>Send a thank you note</u>. It is incredibly important and the polite thing to do to thank the individual(s) you interviewed for their time. You will be known as someone who takes the extra step and respects everyone's time. Be sure you get a card from everyone you speak with, or at the very least, write their names down. Also, you reiterate your interest in the position. Chapter 8 will walk you through everything you need to know about thank you letters and notes.

5. <u>Don't be a job hunter</u>. Often times you have to ask yourself what the company is interviewing you for and then decide what sort of person would fit that description. Is it someone who is out "hunting for a job" or someone who sees themselves as part of the effort, a team player, who wants to make a difference? If you are the job hunter, it will show because you will often come across as self-centered and use phrases such as "I want" and "I am looking for." To avoid this, think from the viewpoint of the company and find out what they need to try and convey how you will feel that need.

6. <u>Listen carefully</u>. When the interviewer is speaking, make an effort to understand what they are really saying. Listening is not just waiting for your turn to speak. It is also watching body language and listening for vocal tone. And with listening comes eye contact. Maintain good eye contact through the entire conversation, or stare at the person's "third eye," the area right in between the eyes.

7. <u>Be honest</u>. At the end of it all, interviewers can cross-check the information you mention in the interview.

8. <u>Speak succinctly</u>. Be confident, enthusiastic, and articulate what you are trying to say. Avoid rambling, but also saying too

little. Give the whole picture, but get to the point as well. Just as you would avoid slang in your cover letter and resume, do the same while speaking.

REFLECT

After the interview, determine whether this position is a "fit" for you.
- Are the people you met with represent the kinds of people you would like to work with?
- Does the organization seem dynamic and energized or do the employees seem lethargic?
- Has the organization met its obligations in terms of agreements and promises made during the interviewing process?

CHAPTER 5

175 Possible Interview Questions You May Encounter

You should never come to an interview completely cold turkey so here is an extensive list of questions that you may be asked. Take the time to read through them to prepare possible answers to them. Yes, it is always possible you will be asked questions that are not on this list. This list is not intended to encompass everything you will be asked, but more so to prepare you for the type of questioning you can expect. If you are confident with this extensive list then you should have no problem answering anything that comes up on an interview.

1. What's your biggest accomplishment so far? What are you most proud of?
2. Why should I hire you?
3. How do you handle a job that's very stressful?
4. Why do you think you will fit in with the company culture? (Research the company, the position you're applying for, etc. before the interviews.)

5. How do you define success? Are you now successful?
6. Why do you want a job here instead of with our competitor?
7. Do you work better on your own or as part of a team?
8. Tell me about a time when you received criticism. How did you handle it?
9. Have you ever lost your job? Why?
10. What will you do if you have a serious difference of opinion with your immediate superior?
11. What have you accomplished in the last five years?
12. Describe what you think this type of job entails and what you might like and dislike about the work.
13. Tell me about a time when you saw room for improvement in some area of your work environment or a process that could be more efficient. What did you do to change the status quo?"
14. Describe an occasion when you had two bosses ask you to do conflicting tasks. How did you handle this dilemma?
15. Describe a time when your supervisor or a co-worker asked you to help out and doing so required extra work outside your established responsibilities or staying later than you anticipated. What did you do, and how did you feel?
16. Tell me about a time when your job required you to perform a task that you didn't know how to do. How did you respond?
17. While at work, a co-worker complains to you about the office manager and some of the office policies and procedures, concluding with "Don't you think so too?" How would you respond
18. What are your strengths?
19. Who was your favorite manager and why?
20. What kind of personality do you work best with and why?

21. Why do you want this job?
22. Where would you like to be in your career five years from now?
23. Tell me about your proudest achievement.
24. If you were at a business lunch and you ordered a rare steak and they brought it to you well done, what would you do?
25. If I were to give you this salary you requested but let you write your job description for the next year, what would it say?
26. Why is there fuzz on a tennis ball?
27. How would you go about establishing your credibility quickly with the team?
28. If you could be anywhere in the world right now, where would you be?
29. How would you feel about working for someone who knows less than you?
30. Was there a person in your career who really made a difference?
31. What's your ideal company?
32. What attracted you to this company?
33. What are you looking for in terms of career development?
34. What do you look for in terms of culture -- structured or entrepreneurial?
35. What do you like to do?
36. Give examples of ideas you've had or implemented.
37. What are your lifelong dreams?
38. What do you ultimately want to become?
39. How would you describe your work style?
40. Tell me about a time where you had to deal with conflict on the job.
41. What would be your ideal working situation?
42. What did you like least about your last job?

43. What do you think of your previous boss?
44. When were you most satisfied in your job?
45. What can you do for us that other candidates can't? What makes you stand out?
46. What are three positive things your last boss would say about you?
47. What opportunities for improvement would your last boss say about you?
48. What were the responsibilities of your last position?
49. What do you know about this industry?
50. What do you know about our company?
51. How long will it take for you to make a significant contribution?
52. What was the last project you headed up, and what was its outcome?
53. What kind of goals would you have in mind if you got this job?
54. Give me an example of a time that you felt you went above and beyond the call of duty at work.
55. Have you ever been on a team where someone was not pulling their own weight? How did you handle it?
56. What is your personal mission statement?
57. Tell me about a time when you had to give someone difficult feedback. How did you handle it?
58. What is your greatest failure, and what did you learn from it?
59. What irritates you about other people, and how do you deal with it? What are your pet peeves?
60. Who has impacted you most in your career, and how?
61. What do you see yourself doing within the first 30 days of this job?
62. What's the most important thing you've learned in school?

63. What three character traits would your friends use to describe you?
64. What will you miss about your present/last job?
65. If you were interviewing someone for this position, what traits would you look for?
66. List five words that describe your character.
67. If I were your supervisor and asked you to do something that you disagreed with, what would you do?
68. Do you think a leader should be feared or liked?
69. What's the most difficult decision you've made in the last two years?
70. Why are you leaving your present job?
71. How do you feel about taking no for an answer?
72. Give me an example of a time you did something wrong. How did you handle it?
73. Tell me the difference between good and exceptional.
74. Why did you choose your major?
75. What are the qualities of a good leader? A bad leader?
76. What is your biggest regret, and why?
77. If you found out your company was doing something against the law, like fraud, what would you do?
78. What assignment was too difficult for you, and how did you resolve the issue?
79. If I were to ask your last supervisor to provide you additional training or exposure, what would she suggest?
80. Describe how you would handle a situation if you were required to finish multiple tasks by the end of the day, and there was no conceivable way that you could finish them.
81. What techniques and tools do you use to keep yourself organized?
82. If you had to choose one, would you consider yourself a big-picture person or a detail-oriented person?

83. If selected for this position, can you describe your strategy for the first 90 days?
84. Why did you leave your last job?
85. What are your long range and short range goals and objectives?
86. What specific goals other than those related to your occupation,
87. have you established for yourself for the next ten years?
88. What do you see yourself doing five years from now? Ten years from now?
89. What do you really want to do in life?
90. How do you plan to achieve your career goals?
91. What are the most important rewards you expect in your career?
92. Why did you choose this career?
93. Can you explain this gap in your employment history?
94. How well do you work with people? Do you prefer working alone or in teams?
95. Have you ever had difficulty with a supervisor? How did you resolve the conflict?
96. What's more important to you -- the work itself or how much you're paid for doing it.
97. Describe the best job you've ever had.
98. Describe the best supervisor you've ever had.
99. What motivates you to go the extra mile on a project or job?
100. What makes you qualified for this position?
101. What qualifications do you have that make you successful in this career?
102. How do you determine or evaluate success?
103. What do you think it takes to be successful in a company like ours?

104. In what ways do you think you can make a contribution to our company?
105. Do you consider yourself a leader?
106. Describe the workload in your current (or most recent) job.
107. Which is more important: creativity or efficiency? Why?
108. Describe the relationship that should exist between the supervisor and those reporting to him or her?
109. Describe the most rewarding experience of your career thus far.
110. Do you have plans for continued study? An advanced degree?
111. In what kind of work environment are you most comfortable?
112. How do you work under pressure?
113. Are you good at delegating tasks?
114. What's one of the hardest decisions you've ever had to make?
115. How well do you adapt to new situations?
116. Why did you decide to seek a position at this company?
117. What can you tell us about our company?
118. What interests you about our products?
119. What do you know about our competitors?
120. What two or three things are most important to you in your job?
121. Are you seeking employment in a company of a certain size? Why?
122. What are your expectations regarding promotions and salary increases?
123. What criteria are you using to evaluate the company for which you hope to work?

124. Do you have a geographic preference? Why?
125. Why do you think you might like to live in the community in which our company is located?
126. What major problem have you encountered and how did you deal with it?
127. What have you learned from your mistakes?
128. What have you accomplished that shows your initiative and willingness to work?
129. Describe a situation in which you were able to use persuasion to successfully convince someone to see things your way.
130. Describe a time when you were faced with a stressful situation that demonstrated your coping skills.
131. Give me a specific example of a time when you used good judgment and logic in solving a problem.
132. Give me an example of a time when you set a goal and were able to meet or achieve it.
133. Tell me about a time when you had to use your presentation skills to influence someone's opinion.
134. Give me a specific example of a time when you had to conform to a policy with which you did not agree.
135. Please discuss an important written document you were required to complete.
136. Tell me about a time when you had to go above and beyond the call of duty in order to get a job done.
137. Give me an example of a time when you had to make a split second decision.
138. What is your typical way of dealing with conflict? Give me an example.
139. Tell me about a time you were able to successfully deal with another person even when that individual may not have personally liked you (or vice versa).

140. Tell me about a difficult decision you've made in the last year.
141. Give me an example of a time when something you tried to accomplish and failed.
142. Give me an example of when you showed initiative and took the lead.
143. Tell me about a recent situation in which you had to deal with a very upset customer or co-worker.
144. Give me an example of a time when you motivated others.
145. Tell me about a time when you delegated a project effectively.
146. Give me an example of a time when you used your fact-finding skills to solve a problem.
147. Tell me about a time when you missed an obvious solution to a problem.
148. Describe a time when you anticipated potential problems and developed preventive measures.
149. Tell me about a time when you were forced to make an unpopular decision.
150. Describe a time when you set your sights too high (or too low).
151. How does this assignment fit into your overall career plan?
152. Describe your management style.
153. What do you believe is the most difficult part of being a supervisor of people?
154. Why are you looking for a new career?
155. What were the five most significant accomplishments in your last assignment?
156. What were the five most significant accomplishments in your career so far?
157. Can you work well under deadlines or pressure?

158. Have you kept up in your field with additional training?
159. If you took the job what would you hope to accomplish in the first year?
160. What questions didn't I ask that you expected?
161. When did you decide on this career?
162. Describe a situation in which you were successful.
163. What do you think it takes to be successful in this career?
164. Would your rather work with information or with people?
165. Are you a goal-oriented person?
166. What major problem have you had to deal with recently?
167. Why did you choose to attend your college?
168. What changes would you make at your college?
169. How has your education prepared you for your career?
170. What were your favorite classes? Why?
171. Do you enjoy doing independent research?
172. Who were your favorite professors? Why?
173. How much training do you think you'll need to become a productive employee?
174. What do you know about our company?
175. Why are you interested in our company?
176. How do you handle a job that's very stressful?

CHAPTER 6
Answering Interview Questions

In this chapter you will find a plethora of questions that you may be asked with some suggested ways to answer them. Use these as a template for when you craft your own answers.

DESCRIBE YOUR EMPLOYMENT HISTORY
What they're wanting to know
- Name of companies you worked for
- Your job titles
- Starting and end dates
- What your job entailed

How to prepare
- Review your resume

WHAT WERE YOUR EXPECTATIONS FOR THE JOB?
What they're wanting to know
- What were your expectations for the job?
- To what extent were these expectations met?

How to prepare
- Discuss what you expected when you took the job
- Examples of how the position worked out for you
- Focus on the job itself, not the company, boss, or your coworkers
- Focus on the highlights and be specific

Example
- If your job involved creating web applications using Cold Fusion, discuss the specific programs you developed and the responsibilities you were given.
- If you were provided training and opportunities for professional development to help you achieve your goals, mention that, as well.

WHAT WERE YOUR RESPONSIBILITIES?

What they're wanting to know
- Are your past experiences related to what they are looking for?
- How have your job responsibilities progressed over time?

How to prepare
- Describe your responsibilities in detail and connect them to the job you are interviewing for
- Tie your responsibilities with the ones listed on the job description
- Be honest

WHAT MAJOR PROBLEMS OR CHALLENGES DID YOU FACE? HOW DID YOU HANDLE THEM?

What they're wanting to know
- Your past behavior is a good indication of your future behavior

- How you problem solve

How to prepare
- Include specific examples
- Discuss researching the issue and contributing to finding a solution
- Consider small mistakes with positive lessons learned

Example
- During a difficult financial period, I was able to satisfactorily negotiate repayment schedules with multiple vendors.
- When the software development of our new product stalled, I coordinated the team which managed to get the schedule back on track. We were able to successfully troubleshoot the issues and solve the problems, within a very short period of time.
- A long-term client was about to take their business to a competitor. I met with the customer and was able to change how we handled the account on a day-to-day basis, in order to keep the business.
- I worked too far ahead of colleagues on a project and thus threw off our coordination efforts

WHAT DID YOU LIKE OR DISLIKE ABOUT YOUR PREVIOUS JOB?

What they're wanting to know
- What is your predisposition like (negative vs optimistic)
- Better understand if this will be a good cultural fit

How to prepare
- What are you looking for in this role

Example
- I enjoyed the people I worked with. It was a friendly and fun atmosphere and I actually enjoyed going into work each morning. I felt the leadership team was great as well. They knew all of their employees on a first name basis and tried to make those personal connections. I also enjoyed that fact that the office tired to do community outreach with local organizations. One of the reasons I am leaving is that I felt I was not challenged enough at the job. As a fresh face in the working world, the company offers a great opportunity for a good entry level position, however, after being there for so many years, I felt I was not able to reach my full potential because of the lack of challenge and there was no room for advancement in the company. While I did enjoy working there and appreciate the skills I developed while with the company, I feel my skill set can be better utilized elsewhere, where my capabilities are more recognized and there is the opportunity for growth.

WHAT WAS MOST REWARDING?
What they're wanting to know
- How engaged & happy you will be based on what you liked/disliked in the past

How to prepare
- What tasks were most rewarding at your current/last job?

WHAT WAS LEAST REWARDING?
What they're wanting to know
- How engaged & happy you will be based on what you liked/disliked in the past

How to prepare
- Avoid discussing past responsibilities that will be a major part of the new job
- Focus on the positives and don't dwell too much on the negatives

Example
- If the last job you had involved extensive customer service telephone work that you hated, and if being on the phone doing something similar is even a minor part of the new job, don't mention it

WHAT WAS YOUR BIGGEST ACCOMPLISHMENT?

What they're wanting to know
- What you accomplished, and what you didn't

How to prepare
- Specific examples of your accomplishments that directly relates to the job you're interviewing
- Only mention <u>minor</u> failures

Example
- If you are interviewing for a job at a school where you will need to manage student registration, explain to the interviewer how you registered students for courses, designed and managed registration software, and solved customer problems.
- If you were working on a project that was behind deadline, explain to the interviewer how you adjusted the workload and the timeline to get back on track and ahead of schedule.

TELL ME ABOUT A TIME WHEN YOU HAD TO DEAL WITH A CO-WORKER WHO WASN'T DOING HIS/HER

FAIR SHARE OF THE WORK. WHAT DID YOU DO AND WHAT WAS THE OUTCOME?

What they're wanting to know
- If you're a team player

How to prepare
- Take a few seconds before answering a difficult question

Example
- I worked closely with Ann who, for the most part, always carried her fair share of the workload. During a stressful time, working on a project with a deadline, I realized Ann's contributions to the project were almost minimal. I made the decision to wait until after the project to speak with her. I'm glad I did, because I learned she'd been going through a very tough time in her personal life and she appreciated my willingness to go the extra mile so the project was completed on time. As a result, our ability to work well together significantly increased.

GIVE ME AN EXAMPLE OF A TIME WHEN YOU TOOK THE TIME TO SHARE A CO-WORKER'S OR SUPERVISOR'S ACHIEVEMENTS WITH OTHERS?

What they're wanting to know
- If you're a team player

How to prepare
- Think about a group project or team effort you were part of

Example
- At my most recent position, one of my coworkers, Dan, did an outstanding job of calming an irate customer, solving the customer's problem and completing a sale. When our boss asked me how things

- Focus on an opportunity that you offered your help with and/or you were asked by someone else because of specific skills you have

Example
  - Most recently, we had a new hire (Paul) that was really struggling with getting to work on time, and I knew the boss (Harry) was getting irritated. Over lunch one day I explained to Paul how important it was to our boss for everyone to be there at least 10 minutes early. It was personal with the Harry, but you could really get on his bad side when you were frequently late. The new employee was grateful for the advice. At his previous employment, the boss was only concerned about the work getting done on time; he/she did not "watch the clock".

TELL ME ABOUT A TIME THAT YOU MISJUDGED A PERSON.

What they're wanting to know
  - If you're a team player
  - If you can see situations from someone else's perspective

How to prepare
  - Take a few seconds before answering a difficult question
  - Consider positive stories over negative ones when possible

Example
  - There was a long-time employee at my company who was very gruff when he spoke to me. At first, I went out of my way to win his approval. Then I realized that was compounding the problem. So I observed how he interacted with other employees and discovered I

wasn't alone. He was gruff to most people. I quit trying to gain his approval and, in the process, discovered he'd learned his behavior from a former boss he'd had whom he admired.

HOW DO YOU GET ALONG WITH EXPERIENCED CO-WORKERS?

What they're wanting to know
- If you're a team player

How to prepare
- Take a few seconds before answering a difficult question

Example
- There are times when I just know that a new way of doing something makes more sense to me; but, first hand, I learned that my "better way" may not be the best way to get the job done. As a consequence, I respect my experienced coworkers knowledge and I've learned how to make a suggestion at the appropriate time.

WHAT WAS IT LIKE WORKING FOR YOUR SUPERVISOR?

What they're wanting to know
- How you get along with your boss

How to prepare
- Do not talk too much (or at all) about bad bosses
- Accentuate the positive

were going, I told him everything was going fine and that Dan had just completed calming an irate customer and closing a sale. It was a win-win-win- for our boss, Dan and the customer.

TELL ME ABOUT A TIME THAT YOU DIDN'T WORK WELL WITH A SUPERVISOR. WHAT WAS THE OUTCOME AND HOW WOULD YOU HAVE CHANGED THE OUTCOME? HAVE YOUR EVER HAD A CONFLICT WITH A BOSS OR PROFESSOR? HOW WAS IT RESOLVED?

What they're wanting to know
- If you're a team player

How to prepare
- Take a few seconds before answering a difficult question
- Focus on the behavioral process for resolving the conflict and working collaboratively
- It's never a problem, but always a lack of communication

Example
- Yes, I have had conflicts in the past. Never major ones, but there have been disagreements that needed to be resolved. I've found that when conflict occurs, it helps to fully understand the other person's perspective, so I take time to listen to their point of view, then I seek to work out a collaborative solution. For example...

HAVE YOU WORKED WITH SOMEONE YOU DIDN'T LIKE? IF SO, HOW DID YOU HANDLE IT?

What they're wanting to know
- If you're a team player

How to prepare
- Take a few seconds before answering a difficult question
- Discuss the communication efforts used to resolve the situation
- Focus on the work the individual did

Example
- Yes, I've worked with someone whom I found difficult to like as a person. However, when I focused on the skills they brought to the job, their ability to solve problems and the two things I did appreciate, slowly my attitude towards them changed. We were never friends, but we did work well together.
- In my last three jobs I have worked with men and women from very diverse backgrounds and cultures. The only time I had difficulty was with people who were dishonest about work issues. I worked with one woman who was taking credit for work that her team accomplished. I had an opportunity to talk with her one day and explained how she was affecting the morale. She became very upset that others saw her that way, and said she was unaware of her behavior or the reactions of others. Her behavior changed after our talk. What I learned from that experience is that sometimes what we perceive about others is not always the case if we check it out.

TELL ME ABOUT A TIME THAT YOU HELPED SOMEONE.

What they're wanting to know
- If you're a team player

How to prepare
- Discuss the situation and why you felt the need to help

WHAT DO YOU EXPECT FROM A SUPERVISOR? WHAT QUALITIES DO YOU FEEL A SUCCESSFUL MANAGER SHOULD HAVE?

What they're wanting to know
- The type of support you expect from your boss

How to prepare
- Highlight positive attributes
- Use an example of someone in your life who has impacted you and helped in your personal development
- Qualities to discuss can include knowledge, a sense of humor, fairness, and loyalty to those who report to them.

Example
- I appreciate a work environment where supervisors try to make personal connections with their employees.
- In my last job, I liked the fact that management did not show favoritism and they were understanding of employees needs, as well as their strengths. Of course, these things take time to know, but I would want my supervisor to try to know me in that way.
- I would like to be able to go to my manager if I have an issue or idea and to be able to feel comfortable to expressing my thoughts. I would also expect my supervisor to be open and honest with me and to let me know if there is anything I could do to improve upon or do differently in my work.
- The key quality in a successful manager should be leadership-- the ability to be the visionary for the people who are working under them. The person who can set the course and direction for their subordinates.

The highest calling of a true leader is inspiring others to reach the highest of their abilities. I'd like to tell you about a person whom I consider to be a true leader...

WHO WAS YOUR BEST BOSS AND WHO WAS THE WORST?
<u>What they're wanting to know</u>
- If you assess blame or carry a grudge

<u>How to prepare</u>
- Take a few seconds before answering a difficult question
- Focus on the positive as much as possible
- When it comes to a negative trait, focus on something small and could be changed easily

<u>Example</u>
- I've learned from each boss I've had. From the good ones, what to do, from the challenging ones - what not to do.
- Early in my career, I had a mentor who helped me a great deal, we still stay in touch. I've honestly learned something from each boss I've had.

WHY ARE YOU LEAVING (WHY HAVE YOU LEFT) YOUR CURRENT POSITION?
<u>What they're wanting to know</u>
- What happened

<u>How to prepare</u>
- Be direct and focus on the future
- Don't speak badly about your previous employer
- Never refer to a major problem with management or speak ill of supervisors, coworkers, or the organization

- Stay focused and clear about your circumstances and future goals

Example
- I found myself bored with the work and looking for more challenges. I am an excellent employee and I didn't want my unhappiness to have any impact on the job I was doing for my employer.
- There isn't room for growth with my current employer and I'm ready to move on to a new challenge.
- I'm looking for a bigger challenge and to grow my career.
- I was laid-off from my last position when our department was eliminated due to corporate restructuring.
- I'm relocating to this area due to family circumstances and left my previous position in order to make the move.
- I've decided that is not the direction I want to go in my career and my current employer has no opportunities in the direction I'd like to head.
- After several years in my last position, I'm looking for an company where I can contribute and grow in a team-oriented environment.
- I am interested in a new challenge and an opportunity to use my technical skills and experience in a different capacity than I have in the past.
- I recently received my degree and I want to utilize my educational background in my next position.
- I am interested in a job with more responsibility, and I am very ready for a new challenge.

- I left my last position in order to spend more time with my family. Circumstances have changed and I'm more than ready for full-time employment again.
- I am seeking a position with a stable company with room for growth and opportunity for advancement.
- I was commuting to the city and spending a significant amount of time each day on travel. I would prefer to be closer to home.
- This position seemed like an excellent match for my skills and experience, which I feel I am not able to fully utilize in my present job.
- The company was cutting back and, unfortunately, my job was one of those eliminated.

HOW DO YOU HANDLE STRESS/PRESSURE?
What they're wanting to know
- How you react to uncertain situations and pressures

How to prepare
- Give examples of how you have handled stress in the past

Example
- Stress is very important to me. With stress, I do the best possible job. The appropriate way to deal with stress is to make sure I have the correct balance between good stress and bad stress. I need good stress to stay motivated and productive.
- I react to situations, rather than to stress. That way, the situation is handled and doesn't become stressful.
- I actually work better under pressure and I've found that I enjoy working in a challenging environment.

- Prioritizing my responsibilities so I have a clear idea of what needs to be done when, has helped me effectively manage pressure on the job.

WHAT MOTIVATES YOU? HOW DO YOU LIKE TO BE REWARDED FOR GOOD PERFORMANCE?

What they're wanting to know
- The key to your success

How to prepare
- Examples of what motivates you
- Enthusiasm in what you like(d) best about your job
- Talk about things like challenges, achievements, and/or recognition

Example
- I was responsible for several projects where I directed development teams and implemented repeatable processes. The teams achieved 100% on-time delivery of software products. I was motivated both by the challenge of finishing the projects ahead of schedule and by managing the teams that achieved our goals.
- I've always been motivated by the desire to do a good job at whatever position I'm in. I want to excel and to be successful in my job, both for my own personal satisfaction and for my employer.
- I have always wanted to ensure that my company's clients get the best customer service I can provide. I've always felt that it's important, both to me personally, and for the company and the clients, to provide a positive customer experience.

WHAT TYPE OF WORK ENVIRONMENT DO YOU PREFER?

What they're wanting to know
- If you this will be a good cultural fit

How to prepare
- Ask them about their current environment
- Use their key words and phrases to describe your preferred environment

Example
- I can be flexible when it comes to my work environment. What is the environment in the Engineering department here at RRS, Inc?

DESCRIBE A DIFFICULT WORK SITUATION/PROJECT AND HOW YOU OVERCAME IT.

What they're wanting to know
- How you handle difficult situations
- How you behave in the past is a general predictor of how you will behave in the future

How to prepare
- Examples of difficult situations and what you did to resolve the situation
- Keep answers positive
- Think about special situations or projects
- Focus on stories of successful resolution

Example
- Even though it was difficult when Jane quit without notice, we were able to rearrange the department workload to cover the position until a replacement was hired

TELL ME ABOUT A TIME THAT YOU WORKED CONVEYING TECHNICAL INFORMATION TO A NONTECHNICAL AUDIENCE.

What they're wanting to know
- The interviewer wants to know how you relate to people outside your area of expertise

How to prepare
- Give examples when you had to explain a difficult concept or topic to someone outside of your area of expertise

Example
- While I worked in the accounting department, I was selected to explain the financial section of the employee's paycheck to all new hires. After my first two sessions, I realized I needed to reframe my information so the new hires would have an accurate understanding of the impact of their decisions as it related to their pay. I worked with colleagues in human resources and marketing, and developed a training outline that was implemented at the other locations throughout the company.

WHY DO YOU THINK YOU WILL BE SUCCESSFUL AT THIS JOB?

What they're wanting to know
- The interviewer is concerned as to whether you see this as a career move, or stop-gap employment

How to prepare
- Focus on the skills and knowledge you bring
- Consider answering with thing like you set personal high standards for yourself and meeting them, you have strong outcomes that are related to your

successes, and/or your boss telling you that you are successful in your job

Example
- As my resume reflects, I have been successful at each of my previous places of employment. My research of your company, the job description outlined, and the information we've exchanged today, lead me to believe I have the skills and experience for which you are looking; and I'm eager to be a contributing employee.

TELL ME ABOUT A TIME THAT YOU PARTICIPATED IN A TEAM, WHAT WAS YOUR ROLE? ARE YOU A TEAM PLAYER?

What they're wanting to know
- Companies, for the most part, do not want "Lone-Rangers" - - they are looking for employees who will adapt to the company culture and get along with others

How to prepare
- Discuss any teams or group projects you've been part of
- Talk about the strength of the team above the individual

Example
- I headed up a project which involved customer service personnel and technicians. I organized a meeting to get everyone together to brainstorm and get his or her input. From this meeting I drew up a plan, taking the best of the ideas. I organized teams, balancing the mixture of technical and non-technical people. We had a deadline to meet, so I did periodic checks with the teams. After three weeks, we were exceeding expectations, and were able to begin implementation

of the plan. It was a great team effort, and a big success. I was commended by management for my leadership, but I was most proud of the team spirit and cooperation which it took to pull it off
- In high school, I enjoyed playing soccer and performing with the marching band. Each required a different kind of team play, but the overall goal of learning to be a member of a group was invaluable. I continued to grow as team member while on my sorority's debate team and through my advanced marketing class where we had numerous team assignments.
- I have had opportunities in my work, school, and athletics to develop skills as a team player. For example, a recent project...

WHAT IS YOUR PREFERRED WAY TO COMMUNICATE?

What they're wanting to know
- This is a good opportunity to show you understand the importance of adjusting your preferences when necessary

How to prepare
- Talk about different methods of communication you have used successfully

Example
- At home, I enjoy talking on the phone and emails. At work, I follow the established pattern. Each of my bosses, in the past, has had a preferred method I've followed their lead.

DO YOU CHECK VOICEMAIL AND EMAIL WHEN ON VACATION?

What they're wanting to know
- The interviewer is wondering whether they will always be able to find you

How to prepare
- Honestly discuss how you handle the work-life balance

Example
- While on vacation, I can be reached for emergencies; however, I also know the people with whom I work are very capable of making good decisions while I'm away. I understand the importance of recharging my battery.

WHY DO YOU WANT THIS JOB?

What they're wanting to know
- Why are you looking

How to prepare
- Think about your goals and how the company will assist in reaching them

Example
- Having worked through a college business major building decks and porches for neighbors, this entry-level job for the area's most respected home builder has my name on it.
- As a dedicated technician, I like doing essential research. Being part of a breakthrough team is an experience I'd love to repeat.
- This job is a good fit for what I've been interested in throughout my career. It offers a nice mix of short- and long-term activities. My short-term achievements

keep me cranked up and the long-term accomplishments make me feel like a billion bucks.
- I want this job selling theater tickets because I'd be good at it. I'm good at speaking to people and handling cash. I would like a job with regular hours and I'm always on time.
- The work I find most stimulating allows me to use both my creative and research skills. The buzz on this company is that it rewards people who deliver solutions to substantial problems.
- I've been very careful about the companies where I have applied. When I saw the ad for this position, I knew I found what I was looking for. What I can bring to this job is my seven years of experience, and knowledge of the industry, plus my ability to communicate and build customer relationships. That, along with my flexibility and organizational skills, makes me a perfect match for this position. I see some challenges ahead of me here, and that's what I thrive on. I have what you need, and you have what I want.

WHY SHOULD WE HIRE YOU? WHY DO YOU WANT TO WORK HERE?

What they're wanting to know
- Your opinion on why you are a strong candidate
- Validate the interviewer's opinion of you
- Ensure that you are seriously interested in the job

How to prepare
- Give concrete examples of your skills and accomplishments
- Compare the job description with your abilities
- Be positive

- Assess what makes you stand out from others with similar experiences
- Spend time researching the company (see preparation bullets for the next question)
- What can you do for the company?

WHAT DO YOU KNOW ABOUT THIS COMPANY?
<u>What they're wanting to know</u>
- How much research you have done on the company
- How committed you are

<u>How to prepare</u>
- Research all relevant and current information on the company
- Gather the company's mission, vision, and value statements, and determine how your own personal views align with theirs
- Research the company's website
- Google the company
- Find the company on LinkedIn
- Read blogs that mention it
- Check with the career office at your college to find alumni who work for the company

WHAT ARE YOUR GOALS FOR THE FUTURE?
<u>What they're wanting to know</u>
- How does the company fit in with your overall <u>career</u> goals

<u>How to prepare</u>
- Stay relevant to the position and the company
- Avoid any personal goals, such as returning to work or growing your family

Example
- My long-term goals involve growing with a company where I can continue to learn, take on additional responsibilities, and contribute as much of value as I can.
- I see myself as a top performing employee in a well-established organization, like this one. I plan on enhancing my skills and continuing my involvement in [related] professional associations.
- Once I gain additional experience, I would like to move on from a technical position to management.
- In the XYZ Corporation, what is a typical career path for someone with my skills and experiences?
- Within 5 years, I would like to become the very best accountant your company has on staff. I want to work toward becoming the expert that other rely upon. And in doing so, I feel I'll be fully prepared to take on any greater responsibilities which might be presented in the long term. For example, here is what I'm presently doing to prepare myself...

WHAT EXPERIENCE DO YOU HAVE IN THIS FIELD? HOW HAS YOUR EDUCATION PREPARED YOU FOR THIS CAREER?

What they're wanting to know
- How your education or other experiences translate and relate to the position

How to prepare
- Speak to specific experiences
- Focus on the behavioral examples in your college background that align to the required competencies

for the career (refer to chapter 1, the resume, for a website resource)

Example
- My education has focused on not only learning the fundamentals, but also on the practical application of the information learned within those classes. For example, I played a lead role in a class project where we gathered and analyzed best practice data from this industry. The results were...

DO YOU CONSIDER YOURSELF SUCCESSFUL?

What they're wanting to know
- How goal-oriented you are

How to prepare
- Discuss how you have achieved or are completing your degree

Example
- I have set several goals, of which I have met some and are on track to achieve the others

WHAT DO CO-WORKERS SAY ABOUT YOU?

What they're wanting to know
- How other perceive you

How to prepare
- Prepare with a quote or two from co-workers, classmates, or professors
- Use a specific statement or paraphrase

Example
- Jill, a co-worker at XYZ Company, always said I was the hardest worker she had ever known

WHAT HAVE YOU DONE TO IMPROVE YOUR KNOWLEDGE IN THE LAST YEAR?

What they're wanting to know
- How and what do you do to stay abreast of trends in the industry

How to prepare
- Improvement activities that relate to the job
- Self-improvement activities can be mentioned, as long as they focus on the job

Example
- I pride myself on my ability to stay on top of what is happening in my industry. I do a lot of reading, such as… I belong to a couple of professional organizations and network at meetings. I take classes and seminars whenever I can.

TELL ME ABOUT A SUGGESTION YOU HAVE MADE.

What they're wanting to know
- What bright and new ideas can you/do you bring with you

How to prepare
- Use suggestions that were accepted and considered successful

TELL ME ABOUT YOUR DREAM JOB. WHAT ARE YOU LOOKING FOR IN A JOB?

What they're wanting to know
- If the job and/or the company culture is the right fit

How to prepare
- Stay vague
- Avoid discussing a specific job

Example
- A job where I love the work, like the people, can contribute and can't wait to get to work.

HOW WOULD YOUR PREVIOUS SUPERVISOR/PROFESSOR DESCRIBE YOU?
What they're wanting to know
- How your supervisor perceived your performance

How to prepare
- Quotes or paraphrasing works best
- Ask your supervisors and/or professors for letters of recommendations
- Discuss positive qualities, such as loyalty, good energy, positive attitude, taking on leadership opportunities, being a team player, expertise in certain areas, taking initiative, being patient, hard worker, good use of creativity, or being a problem solver.

Example
- I believe she would say I am a very energetic person, that I'm results oriented, and one of the best people she has ever worked with. Actually, I know she would say that, because those are her very words. May I show you a letter of recommendation?

WE ARE READY TO MAKE AN OFFER. ARE YOU READY TO ACCEPT TODAY?
What they're wanting to know
- They don't want you to go away to think about it and change your mind

How to prepare
- Never make a major life decision without thoroughly thinking it through -- 24 hours and good pros & cons list

Example
- Based on my research and the information I have gathered during the interview process, I feel I am in a position to consider an offer. I do, however, have a personal policy that I give myself at least 24 hours to make major life decisions. I could let you know by tomorrow.

CHAPTER 7

73 Questions To Ask The Interviewer

It is always important to ask questions during the interview, which is generally done at the end. You want to ask questions to figure out if the position is the right fit for you and how you will be interacting with the individual and/or team.

Pick and choose from the following list, and add it to your quick sheet:

1. What are the day-to-day responsibilities of this job? What do you consider the five most important day-to-day responsibilities of this job? Why?
2. What challenges might I encounter if I were to take this position? How do you think these could best be handled?
3. What are the first projects/objectives to be addressed?
4. What are the priorities you'd like addressed in the first six months to a year?
5. What major issue(s) is the functional group facing right now?

6. Are there any gaps or improvement opportunities in particular you are looking to address?
7. What personality traits do you consider critical to success in this job? What type of person are you seeking?
8. How is performance measured? Based on the individual or a team measurement?
9. What might be a logical or natural career path/progression for someone in this role?
10. Assuming I excelled in the position, what opportunities for growth and development might I expect?
11. What is the timetable for filling the position?
12. What are the next steps in the interview process?
13. Will you be contacting all candidates regardless of the outcome?
14. What key results do you expect out of someone in this position?
15. Why is this position open at this point in time?
16. How much independence would I have in making decisions?
17. What key factors contribute to success in this job?
18. Are there any major changes due to take place at the company in the near future?
19. How would you like the new person to do things differently from the person who had this position earlier?
20. What factors have been responsible for the company's success in the past?
21. Can you please tell me how your career has developed at Happy Corp. and would someone entering the company today have similar opportunities?
22. I read in your literature that your training program is comprised of three (3) six month rotations. Does the employee have any input into where s/he will go at the end

of each rotation? How do you evaluate the employee's performance during the training period?
23. I read in Business Week that a major competitor, Eager Corp., is increasing its market share in your main market. What plans does your firm have to regain its lost market share?
24. What would a typical working day be in this position? Can you describe for me what a work week is like?
25. How often has it been filled in the past five years? What were the main reasons?
26. What is most pressing? What would you like to have done in the next 3 months.
27. What are some of the long term objectives you would like to see completed?
28. What type of support does this position receive in terms of people, finances. etc?
29. What freedom would I have in determining my own work objectives, deadlines, and methods of measurement?
30. What accounts for success within the company?
31. What can you tell me more about the department?
32. What is your management style?
33. How would you describe your company culture?
34. What benefits are provided to your employees?
35. What type of internal and external training do you provide? Do you support continuous development?
36. How are performance appraisals conducted within your organization?
37. What is your organization's commitment to diversity?
38. What is your retention rate within the company? Within the hiring department?
39. When will you be making a decision on this position?
40. What are the most important skills and attributes you are looking for in filling this position?

41. How many hours of work per week would be required to be successful?
42. What is the organization structure of your department?
43. How do the organizational values influence your decision-making?
44. What is your vision for your department over the next two to three years?
45. What major challenges are you currently facing as a manager?
46. What is your competitive advantage in the marketplace?
47. What makes your company better than your competitors?
48. What are the areas where your competitors are better than your company?
49. Who do you consider your customers to be?
50. Can you tell me more about the other people in the department/organization I would be working with?
51. What would you consider to be exceptional performance from someone performing in this position in the first 90 days?
52. What is your preferred method of communicating with your team?
53. What can the person in this position do to make you successful?
54. How long have you been with the organization?
55. What has been your career path within the organization?
56. What are the organizational goals?
57. What are the metrics used to measure whether or not you are achieving your goals?
58. How far out into the future is the organization planning?
59. How are new strategic initiatives communicated to the organization?
60. What is your approach with regard to the use of technology?
61. What is the interviewing style of the person I will be interviewing with?
62. Who has final hiring decision authority?
63. Why did you decide to join this company?
64. Were your expectations initially met?

65. Have your expectations changed over time?
66. Tell me about a typical working day for you.
67. How many hours a day do you typically work?
68. How much travel is involved in your job?
69. What do you consider to be your company's greatest strengths and weaknesses?
70. What do you like about working here?
71. What don't you like about working here and what would you change?
72. When can I expect to hear from you?
73. Are there any other questions I can answer for you?

CHAPTER 8
Thank You Letters

This is an important aspect after your interview that you cannot miss. It can make you stand out from the other interviewee's. You want to send out a thank you letter as soon as you get back from the interview that day or no later than the following day. It is acceptable to send an emailed thank you letter if it matches the job, company, and communication standards. However, you may want to consider a simple, hand-written, snail-mail thank you note as it will make you stand out from the crowd who emails. A thank you note is your opportunity to reiterate your interest, sills, and what you can bring to the company.

FORMATTING A THANK YOU EMAIL

Begin by formatting the thank you as you would a formal letter.

Hired!

Date

Dear Mr./Ms. last name

Use the first paragraph to thank the interviewer for taking the time to meet with you. Mention your interest in the job and how enthusiastic you are about it.

The second paragraph of your thank you letter should include the reasons why you are an excellent candidate for the job. List specific skills that relate to the job you interviewed for. The more detailed you are, the more the interviewer will know about your qualifications. Circle back to certain points you talked about at the interview.

The third paragraph (optional) can be used to mention anything that you didn't bring up at the interview that you think is important for the employer to know.

In your closing paragraph, reiterate your appreciation for being considered for the job and let the interviewer know you are looking forward to hearing from him or her soon. You also may want to mention that if they need any additional information, you'll make it available. Conclude by saying you look forward to hearing from them soon.

Sincerely,

Your name.

FORMATTING A THANK YOU NOTE

This should be something simple and hand written. You want to thank them for their time and consideration, express how much you like the company, and you continue to be interested in the job following your meeting. Also, if the interview was pretty relaxed and the interviewer referred to themselves by first name, don't hesitate to start the note with: Dear [First Name]. Remember, you want this to be hand written and separate from the official letter you send out. You can buy cheap thank you cards at discount stores such as Target, Wal-Mart, and even the dollar store!

CHAPTER 9
Following Up

If you had a great interview and didn't hear back by their stated time, you need to take it upon yourself to follow up. Do not follow up sooner than what the interviewer tells you. Balance the aggressiveness of your follow-up with the field you are in; the more aggressive the job is, the more aggressive you should be in following up (Example: If you're in sales, you probably should be following up every 2-3 days, unless otherwise stated). One fact to consider -- many companies don't tell you their hiring decision (unless you're the one they're hiring), rude though that practice may be. They hope you will just give up and go away after some time. If no one returns your emails or voicemails after several weeks, let it go and presume that there will be no offer.

EMAIL

Email can be a great tool for following up.

You want to use email when:
1. Quick action matters. The job could be filled while you're waiting for postal mail to be delivered.
2. That was the way you sent your resume and especially if the employer requested electronic communication in a job ad.
3. You are dealing with a high-tech firm. The firm's hiring authority probably doesn't use paper is and may think voicemail is a bother

Keep your email follow-up short and send it in plain text in the body of the email, not as an attachment. Use appropriate business language and don't forget your contact information, even though the interviewer can push the reply button and get back to you with ease.

For Example:
>Good Afternoon, Dave,
>
>That interview with you was great! Thanks again. Just wanted you to know that I am very interested in [position] with [name of company]. Please call or email me with an update at your earliest convenience.
>
>Sincerely,
>
>Bob Smith

PHONE CALLS

If you call interviewers too often you may waste their prime work hours, annoy them, and probably jeopardize your opportunity for the job. Space your follow-up calls to once a week and fill in the slack with e-mails. Avoid calling during prime working hours, so aim for early morning or at the end of the workday. Your conversation should look something like:

> Hi, this is [your name]. How are you doing, [interviewer]? I interviewed with you on [week day]. Since I am very interested in this opportunity, I thought I should follow-up with you. You thought you might have an answer on [day]. How is your decision process going?

You want to avoid leaving messages if possible, but if you tried several times, that may be your only option. Be sure to give them a 30 second clip of something interesting. For example:

> This is [name]. I'm calling about the [job title or department] opening. After reflecting on some of the issues you mentioned during our meeting, I thought of a facet of one problem you might like to know [create intrigue]. My number is xxx-xxx-xxxx.

EASY CONVERSATION OPENERS
Use the following starters to warm up the individual to the conversation:
1. Is this a good time to talk?
2. I think you'll be interested to know _____.
3. I understand you're still reviewing many applications.
4. I forgot to go into the key details of [something mentioned during the interview] that might be important to you.

5. While listening to you, I neglected to mention my experience in [function]. It was too important for me to leave out, since the position calls for substantial background in that area.
6. I was impressed with your _____.
7. I appreciate your emphasis on _____.

KEEP IT GOING
1. Remind the interviewer why you're so special, what makes you unique (exceptional work in a specific situation, innovating):
2. *Let me review what I'm offering you that's special.*
3. Establish a common denominator --- a work or business philosophy:
4. *It seems like we both approach work in the [name of] industry from the same angle.*
5. Note a shared interest that benefits the employer:
6. *I found a new site that may interest you --- it's XYZ. It reports on the news items we discussed... Would you like the URL?*

CHAPTER 10
Job Offers & Negotiations

When negotiating a job offer, don't just take the salary into consider-- Look at the entire package, including:

- Health benefits (medical, dental, and vision)
- Paid time off and/or sick
- Retirement matching
- Flexible work arrangements
- Short term & long term disability
- Life insurance
- Tuition assistance and/or loan repayment assistance
- Stock options
- Bonuses
- And other perks

Then begin discovering what you're worth by researching salary surveys for your occupation, experience and location. Use sites like salary.com, cbsalary.com, and bls.gov. Be sure you are researching salary in your area and occupation.Go back to chapter 3, Salary requirements, to discover more methods.

If you are asked point-blank about salary, counter by asking what the range is, so you know the boundaries. Follow up by saying you'd expect a salary that's competitive with the market or, if you know the market value, give him a bracketed range.

When everything is done, be sure to get it in writing. Request a job offer letter.

CONSIDERING AN OFFER

You do not have to give your answer the moment the job offer is presented to you, so be prepared to have a quick response on needing to think through the offer.

> *This is great news. I really appreciate the offer. However, this position would mean great changes for me. Is it alright if I get back to you tomorrow/[day of week]?*

If salary/benefits were not what you hoped for
Figure out what is more important to you, then see if you and your potential employer can agree on terms you both can live with.

If you're hoping another job offer would come through
Call the other organization, let them know that you have been offered a position, but wanted to check in before you accepted the other job. Sometimes this will be enough to move the wheels.

If you are not sure about the job/organization
Tactfully bring up any concerns, if you can.

If after everything, you're still not sure, write a list of pro's and con's and then sleep on it.

DECLINING AN OFFER

If you've been interviewing at multiple places and following the steps outlined in this book, you may find yourself with multiple job offers-- a good problem to have. Once you've gone over your pros and cons list and decided on the better fit, you will need to notify the company who will not be winning your employment.

Begin by calling the organization first, and then follow up with a formal letter. It is ok to state that another offer was a better fit for you, but you do not have to provide details as to why. Better fit could've been better for your career goals, your degree application, or your abilities and skills.

Be sure you are polite, brief, and to the point. Include a thanks and appreciation for the offer, followed by a written rejection of the job offer.

CHAPTER 11
Organizing The Search

When you are organizing your job search, choose a method that you are comfortable and familiar with. If you already use Word or Excel to organize your notes, then continue with this method. Maybe you prefer to keep things in a physical notebook or three ring binder. It really doesn't matter <u>how</u> you organize as long as you keep the following information for each job:

1. Job title
2. Job description
3. Organization
4. Date of application
5. Where did you apply? (Site, LinkedIn, Indeed, etc).
6. Link to application (if applicable)
7. User ID & Password for application (if applicable)
8. Version of resume used
9. Date of first interview
    a. With whom?
    b. Thank you note sent?

Hired!

10. Date of second interview
    a. With whom?
    b. Thank you note sent?
11. Additional interviews
    a. With whom
    b. Thank you note sent?
12. If rejected, any feedback?

If a job is no longer viable, cross it out and move on to the next.

CHAPTER 12

Places to Search

Here's a short list of some places to start your job search:

- http://www.indeed.com

- http://www.careerbuilder.com

- http://www.monster.com

- http://www.dice.com (good for IT related jobs)

- http://www.LinkedIn.com

- Check with your college or university

- Join an association group for your interest or career group

CHAPTER 13
Letter of Resignation

Congratulations! You got the job. If you are currently working somewhere, you need to provide a courtesy 2-week notice. It documents the fact that you are leaving to your human resources department, provides the date of your departure, and is a mark of professionalism that allows you to leave your current position without burning any bridges.

Write a simple, brief, and focused letter to your immediate supervisor and be sure to copy human resources in as well. Include your effective resignation date (your last day on the job) and refrain from any criticism about your employer or job. Keep it professional and polite by including a short appreciation for working with the company.

Hired!

Dear [name of supervisor]:
cc: Human Resources

I would like to inform you that I am resigning from my position as [position title] for [company name], effective [date].

Thank you very much for the opportunities for professional and personal development that you have provided me. I have enjoyed working for the organization and appreciate the support provided me during my time here.

If I can be of any help during this transition, please let me know.

Sincerely,
[Your Name]

CHAPTER 14
Informational Interviewing

Out of 200 resumes that are sent in, only 1 will result in a job offer. However, out of every 12 informational interviews, 1 will result in a job offer. Increase your odds and start networking while you're still in school.

Information interviews will help you get a feel of the field or industry you plan on going into. While most people screen jobs and companies after they've already taken a job, informational interviewing provides you the opportunity to conduct the screening process before accepting a position while also establishing a network for yourself.

WHY GO THROUGH THE HASSLE?

1. Gain valuable information about the career field you are interested in and the skills needed to do your job effectively.

2. Get the opportunity to make personal contacts among management-level personnel.
3. Learn what happens on the job beyond the understanding provided through your course work or other outside research
4. Gain confidence in talking with people while learning what you need to know.
5. Gain expose you to a variety of jobs and personalities of companies making the search for your "niche" that much easier.
6. Provides an opportunity to learn where you might fit into a particular organization.

Steps for an informational interview:
1. Identify the occupation(s) you are interested in and make a list of all possible questions you have about it.
2. Identify people in the field: start with your immediate network (friends, family, coworkers, etc) and branch out to alumni of your college. Be sure to do some research before the conversation, such as the organization, person you'll be speaking with, and product produced by the organization.
3. Never ask for a job!! Your #1 intent for these is to better understand what the job, role, and/or industry is like. You may unintentionally gain a mentor or a branch in your network.

SCHEDULING THE INTERVIEW

Letter

Think of it like a cover letter, minus the pitch about yourself. Include:

- A brief introduction about yourself;
- Why you are writing to this individual;
- A brief statement of your interests or experiences in the person's field, organization or location;
- Why you would like to converse. Be straightforward; tell him/her you are asking for information and advice.
- The last paragraph of the letter should always include a sentence about how and when you will contact this person again.

Remember to proofread before sending, and of course follow up!

> Dear Mr./Mrs. [last name],
>
> My name is [your name], and I am a senior year grad student at [University/College]. [Your focus] has been of interest to me since I took a class in that subject as an undergraduate. Your firm/organization has an outstanding reputation in that field of practice.
>
> My area of concentration in school has been [your focus], and I would greatly appreciate the opportunity to meet with you briefly to discuss the practice of your specialty. I am especially interested in your views regarding [interest]. Any further insights you have would be greatly appreciated.

> *Feel free to reach out to me at your earliest convenience if you're able to find time to meet with me. I promise to not take too much of your time!*
>
> *Thank you so much,*
>
> *[Your name]*

Phone

Remember, they are volunteering their time to speak with you, so be respectful and flexible. If they sound too busy on the phone initially, ask if you can call back at a better time.

> *Hello, my name is _____. I'm conducting career research in your field. I would like to meet and talk with you for about 30 minutes so that I can find out more about your field of expertise.*
>
> *Hi, my name is _____ and I'm a student at _____ University. I got your name from _____. You're in a line of work that I'm interested in, and I was hoping that you could help me gain insights into the profession. I'm sure that my questions could be answered in a 20-30-minute informational interview.*

If you prefer to arrange an appointment in person and cannot get past the front desk, treat receptionists as resources. They hold the key to getting inside the unit or section of that organization if you do not already have an inside contact or referral. Ask them some of your questions. You will usually get good information. Receptionists and other support staff know much more about their company than we often realize. They know how it works, the names of key people, and even job requirements. It is important that they understand what you want. If you ask them something that they feel could be more fully answered by someone else, they will usually give you a referral.

Use your own creativity, but most importantly, emphasize that you are simply trying to get first-hand information, and whatever they share with you will be appreciated.

Consider scheduling some of your interviews with managers and supervisors who have the authority to hire. Identify yourself and explain that you are researching careers in the their field, and that you obtained the person's name from _____(if you were referred).

Just like a job interview, you need to come prepared to the informational interview.

Prior to the interview
1. Do your homework: Company Website, Annual Reports, Other Company Literature, Library Reference Material, University Career Service Office
2. Call to confirm your interview and arrive early. Have all of your questions on hand, bring a notebook and pen to jot down notes, **dress appropriately**, and just in case, bring your resume.

Questions to ask
1. What is your job like?
    a. A typical day?
    b. What do you do? What are the duties/functions/responsibilities of your job?
    c. What kinds of problems do you deal with?

      d. What kinds of decisions do you make?
      e. What percentage of your time is spent doing what?
      f. How does the time use vary? Are there busy and slow times or is the work activity fairly constant?
2. How did this type of work interest you and how did you get started?
3. How did you get your job? What jobs and experiences have led you to your present position?
4. Can you suggest some ways a student could obtain this necessary experience?
5. What are the most important personal satisfactions and dissatisfactions connected with your occupation? What part of this job do you personally find most satisfying? Most challenging? What do you like and not like about working in this industry?
6. What things did you do before you entered this occupation?
      a. Which have been most helpful?
      b. What other jobs can you get with the same background?
7. What are the various jobs in this field or organization?
8. Why did you decide to work for this company?
9. What do you like most about this company?
10. Do you find your job exciting or boring? Why?
11. How does your company differ from its competitors?
12. Why do customers choose this company?
13. Are you optimistic about the company's future and your future with the company?
14. What does the company do to contribute to its employees' professional development?

15. How does the company make use of technology for internal communication and outside marketing? (Use of e-mail, Internet, intranets, World Wide Web page, video conferencing, etc.)
16. What sorts of changes are occurring in your occupation?
17. How does a person progress in your field? What is a typical career path in this field or organization?
    a. What is the best way to enter this occupation?
    b. What are the advancement opportunities?
    c. What are the major qualifications for success in this occupation?
18. What were the keys to your career advancement? How did you get where you are and what are your long-range goals?
19. What are the skills that are most important for a position in this field?
20. What particular skills or talents are most essential to be effective in your job? How did you learn these skills? Did you enter this position through a formal training program? How can I evaluate whether or not I have the necessary skills for a position such as yours?
21. How would you describe the working atmosphere and the people with whom you work?
22. Is there a basic philosophy of the company or organization and, if so, what is it? (Is it a people, service or product oriented business?)
23. What can you tell me about the corporate culture?
24. What is the average length of time for an employee to stay in the job you hold? Are there incentives or disincentives for staying in the same job?
25. Is there flexibility related to dress, work hours, vacation schedule, place of residence, etc.?

26. What work-related values are strongest in this type of work (security, high income, variety, independence)?
27. If your job progresses as you like, what would be the next step in your career?
28. If your work were suddenly eliminated, what kinds of work do you feel prepared to do?
29. With the information you have about my education, skills, and experience, what other fields or jobs would you suggest I research further before I make a final decision?
30. How is the economy affecting this industry?
31. What can you tell me about the employment outlook in your occupational field? How much demand is there for people in this occupation? How rapidly is the field growing? Can you estimate future job openings?
32. What obligations does your employer place have on you outside of the ordinary work week? What social obligations go along with a job in your occupation?
    a. Are there organizations you are expected to join?
    b. Are there other things you are expected to do outside work hours?
33. How has your job affected your lifestyle?
34. What are the salary ranges for various levels in this field? Is there a salary ceiling?
35. What are the major rewards aside from extrinsic rewards such as money, fringe benefits, travel, etc.?
36. From your perspective, what are the problems you see working in this field?
37. What are the major frustrations of this job?
38. What interests you least about the job or creates the most stress?

39. If you could do things all over again, would you choose the same path for yourself? Why? What would you change?
40. What are the educational, requirements for this job? What other types of credentials or licenses are required? What types of training do companies offer persons entering this field? Is graduate school recommended? An MBA? Does the company encourage and pay for employees to pursue graduate degrees?
41. Does your work relate to any experiences or studies you had in college?
42. How well did your college experience prepare you for this job?
43. What courses have proved to be the most valuable to you in your work? What would you recommend for me?
44. How important are grades/GPA for obtaining a job in this field?
45. How do you think my university's reputation is viewed when it comes to hiring?
46. How do you think graduation from a private (or public) university is viewed when it comes to hiring?
47. How did you prepare for this work? If you were entering this career today, would you change your preparation in any way to facilitate entry?
48. What abilities or personal qualities do you believe contribute most to success in this field/job?
49. What are the typical entry-level job titles and functions? What entry level jobs are best for learning as much as possible?

50. Who is the department head or supervisor for this job? Where do you and your supervisor fit into the organizational structure?
51. Who else do you know who is doing similar kinds of work or uses similar skills? What other kinds of organizations hire people to perform the functions you do here? Do you know of other people whom I might talk to who have similar jobs?
52. Do you have any advice for someone interested in this field/job? Are there any written materials you suggest I read? Which professional journals and organizations would help me learn more about this field?
53. What kinds of experience, paid or unpaid, would you encourage for anybody pursuing a career in this field?
54. What special advice do you have for a student seeking to qualify for this position?
55. Do you have any special world of warning or encouragement as a result of your experience?
56. These are my strongest assets (skills, areas of knowledge, personality traits and values):_____. Where would they fit in this field? Where would they be helpful in this organization? Where might they fit in other fields? Where might they be helpful in other organizations?
57. How would you assess the experience I've had so far in terms of entering this field?
58. [If you feel comfortable and it seems appropriate:] Would you mind taking a look at my resume?

Remember to share something about yourself (such as your enthusiasm in the career field), but do not dominate the conversation.

Keep in contact with this person. They have invested time talking to you so it is only appropriate that you keep them updated with your progress and research. You never know, they may not have a job for you, but they may know others who do.

Before leaving, ask your contact to suggest names of others who might be helpful to you and ask permission to use your contact's name when contacting these new contacts.

ALWAYS, ALWAYS, ALWAYS send a thank you note within 1-3 days of the interview, just as you would if it was a job interview. Be sure to include:
1. A quote of something that the resource person said back to them, word for word.
2. Ask the person to keep you in mind if they come across any other information that may be helpful to you in your career research.
3. Include your email and phone number under your signature.

Organize everything
1. Keep a folder or notebook dedicated to your informational interviews. This will help you keep everything straight and a good place for you to refer to later on.
2. Evaluate your interview. Asking yourself the following questions:
    a. What did I learn from this interview (both positive and negative impressions)?
    b. How does what I learned fit with my own interests, abilities, goals, values, etc.?

c. What do I still need to know?
d. What plan of action can I make?

> 💡 **QUICK TIPS** 💡
> - If you ask for 20-30 minutes of a person's time, stick to the limit.
> - Take all information given with a grain of salt and don't settle for 1 or 2 interviews about a given area of work. Everyone has different professional paths that led them to their position -- try to get as many different perspectives as possible.
> - Avoid impressions about an area of work based solely on whether the person interviewed was likeable or the surroundings attractive.
> - While at the interview, ask what you want to know but really let the person talk because you might discover and acquire information about unanticipated areas of employment. You don't have to stick strictly to your question outline... this is also good networking practice. Listen to cues and ask questions as you see fit.
> - Note your reactions on an objective level, but don't ignore personal feelings.
> - Find out if the interviewee has any insight on the qualifications necessary for a position such as the one you are discussing.

Talking with people doesn't have to be a formal process or one you practice only when job hunting. Chat with people casually -- on a plane or bus, while waiting in lines, and at social gatherings. Since most people enjoy talking about their work, curiosity can open many doors.

CHAPTER 15

Gaining Experience While In College

I know, I know... it seems silly to think that you have to work and study at the same time, but I promise you that it will only come in handy once you graduate and are out on your own. Working while you're in college doesn't only provide you additional income, but it also gives you something that money can't: experience.

It's a tough world out there. You will have a lot of education (and loans!) when you're done, but there won't be as many jobs available to you. You'll be competing with people with more experience than you for the same jobs. I won't sugar coat this: you'll be backed into a corner and scratching your head because companies won't hire you due to not having enough experience, but you need them to hire you so that you can get that experience. How do you get that experience if they won't hire you? Well, here are 5 easy tips you can do to get that experience while still in college:

1. **Work in the industry that you are most interested in getting into.** Just be honest with yourself: you won't start at the top. You won't be anywhere near the top, but you will be in the industry gaining the experience you'll need to keep going.
2. **Realize that you are *NOT* too good for an entry level position.** Starting at an entry level position while in college will also give you a slight upper hand out of college because you may become qualified for the next step.
3. **Apply for Work-Study programs.** It's a great place to get work while on Federal Assistance, get experience, and network! One of the best things you can do is network with associates not just in the career path that you are interested in, but also those outside of it as well. You never know when those paths will cross.
4. **Get an internship.** Even if you don't get credit for it or it's unpaid, you are still gaining valuable experience and establishing strong networks. Internships give you a small glimpse into the world that you are interested in being a part of. Even if you get an unpaid one, it will still be worth it. In addition to the on-the-job skills you learn, you will also learn incredible skills on how to budget your money and manage your time more effectively.
5. **Network.** Any person you come in contact has the potential to be the key to getting your job. It can be a friend of a friend, someone you met at your local religious group, or a group of people who share the same passions and hobbies. It doesn't matter who or where you meet these people, but establishing that

network and tie with them will help you gain employment in the future.

CHAPTER 16

Finding Opportunities in Rejection

Rejection is hard. It's hard when you studied really hard and ended up getting a bad grade. It's hard when you finally got the courage to ask out that cute girl in English and she tells you she has a boyfriend. And it's hard when the guy you've been talking to tells you he wants to be friends. But what's even harder is after all of the blood, sweat, and tears that you put in to getting your degree, you get the "thanks, but no thanks" generic email from employers.

Rejection during a job search is your opportunity to reevaluate what's going wrong.

1. Are you getting calls for phone interviews?
    a. Yes: congratulations, your resume is working for you
    b. No: time to edit and polish the resume
2. Are you getting call backs for an interview?
    a. Yes: congratulations, your past experience demonstrates you have the skills and behaviors that the organization is looking for

      b. No: time to reevaluate how you're answering those questions and if there's a way you can tie your experiences in with what they're looking for

HINT: If/when you do have those phone screens, try to remember to write down the questions they ask. One, it will give you a chance to think through the question. Two, you'll have a list of questions to work on for future opportunities. Most phone screens will have the same variation of questions.

3. Are you getting the job?
      a. Yes: WOOHOO! You are a superstar.
      b. No: it's time to polish up your interviewing skills.

HINT: Look the part, sound the part, and know the part. Make sure you're dressed appropriately. Make sure you are not being informal. Think through each question they ask you. Do your research on the company, the job, and of course possible interview questions.

Last, but not least, you can always reach out to the recruiter or the hiring manager for feedback, keeping in mind that 99% of the time you may not hear anything back at all. It's not their priority nor do they want to open up a liability. On occasion you may hear something back that is useful. Either way, it never hurts to ask.

www.ingramcontent.com/pod-product-compliance
Lightning Source LLC
Chambersburg PA
CBHW030703220526
45463CB00005B/1882